The World of
The Brontës

Ann Dinsdale

The Brontës are perhaps the world's most famous literary family. Charlotte, Emily and Anne Brontë came to live at Haworth Parsonage as children in 1820, and it was here on the edge of the wild Yorkshire moors that they wrote some of the best-loved books in the English language.

In the years since their first publication, the Brontë novels have been translated into all the world's major languages, and their characters and themes have become part of popular culture. The power of the Brontës' writing, the compelling story of their lives and the wild beauty of their moorland home have enthralled and inspired generations of readers, writers and artists from around the world.

Patrick Brontë

'I do not deny that I am, somewhat eccentrick.'

Patrick Brontë was born on 17 March 1777 (St Patrick's Day), in a two-room cabin at Emdale, in the parish of Drumballyroney, in County Down, Ireland. The family's original name is uncertain and usually appears in surviving records as 'Brunty' or 'Prunty'. Patrick later claimed that as a child he was pointed out as being 'a gentleman by nature', and that this remark had a profound influence on his life. Driven by ambition, he set about acquiring the education which would enable him to leave his humble origins far behind.

Patrick's hard-won education earned him a place at St John's College, Cambridge, where he enrolled as an undergraduate in 1802. Throughout his academic career his abilities attracted the attention of several influential sponsors, including William Wilberforce, the anti-slavery campaigner. This important new phase of Patrick's life was marked by a change of name: he became Brontë instead of Brunty. It has been suggested that he was emulating his hero, Nelson, who had recently been created Duke of Bronte; bronte (*vrontí*) is also the Greek word for thunder, an appropriate choice for a young man at the start of his career.

It seems that Patrick had already decided on a career in the church and, following ordination, he held curacies at Wethersfield in Essex and then Wellington in Shropshire, before moving north to

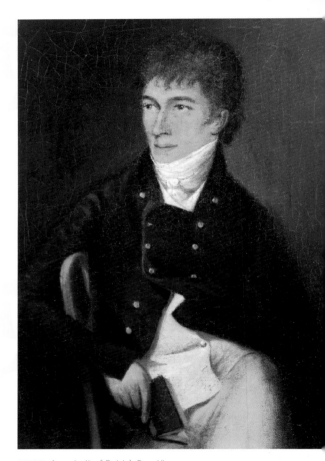

ABOVE A portrait of Patrick Brontë as a young man.

> I do not deny that I am, somewhat eccentrick [sic]. Had I been numbered amongst the calm, sedate, concentric men of the world, I should not have been as I now am, and I should, in all probability, never have had such children as mine have been.
>
> *Patrick Brontë in a letter to Elizabeth Gaskell, 30 July 1857*

Dewsbury, Hartshead-cum-Clifton and Thornton, near Bradford, before his final move to Haworth in 1820.

By the time he arrived in Haworth, Mr Brontë had married Maria Branwell, daughter of a prosperous Cornish merchant, who was visiting relatives in West Yorkshire when they met. Following a whirlwind courtship the couple married and produced six children in rapid succession: Maria (1814), Elizabeth (1815), Charlotte (1816), Patrick Branwell (1817), Emily Jane (1818) and Anne (1820).

Within 18 months of the family's arrival at Haworth, Mrs Brontë died; at the age of 44 Patrick Brontë found himself a widower with six young children to support and a sprawling parish to run. Apart from brief periods away at school, the Brontë sisters shared in Branwell's lessons at home with their father. At a time when too much learning for girls was seen as unnecessary, he encouraged all his children in their eager pursuit of knowledge and was later to tell Elizabeth Gaskell, author of *The Life of Charlotte Brontë* (1857): 'I frequently thought I discovered signs of rising talent which I had seldom, or never before, seen in any of their age.' He was an inspiring father who passed on his love of the arts to his children.

Much of the good Patrick Brontë achieved during his long ministry at Haworth has been overshadowed by his daughters' fame. The many letters and testimonials he wrote on behalf of his parishioners show his practical interest in their welfare. No effort was spared in attempts to improve the lives of the

ABOVE This photograph of Patrick Brontë is one of several images taken late in his life.

villagers, and he would walk great distances to visit far-flung farms and cottages. Mr Brontë's interest in medicine and public health led to his petitioning the General Board of Health to send an inspector to Haworth. As a result, health improvements were gradually introduced, although these came too late to benefit Patrick Brontë's own family.

Having outlived his wife and all of his children, Patrick Brontë died at Haworth Parsonage on 7 June 1861 at the age of 84. He took great pride in his daughters' achievements and lived long enough to experience the first influx of tourists to Haworth, and see souvenir photographs of himself available for sale on Main Street.

BELOW Patrick Brontë's *Cottage Poems* was published in 1811 during his time at Hartshead. His works were intended to offer simple moral guidance to 'the unlearned and poor'. Although they do not possess great literary merit, their influence can be traced in the poetry produced by his children. They also meant that his children grew up familiar with the sight of their own family name in print.

RIGHT A sample of Charlotte Brontë's handwriting, authenticated by her father. After her death in 1855, Mr Brontë cut Charlotte's letters into snippets to meet the many requests from admirers of her books.

Mrs Brontë

'... my heart is more ready to attach itself to earth than heaven.'

Maria Branwell was born on 15 April 1783, one of the eleven children of Thomas Branwell and his wife Anne Carne. Maria's father was a prosperous tea merchant and property owner in Penzance, Cornwall, where the family lived in an elegant house in Chapel Street. She grew up in a very different world from that of her future husband; Penzance was a thriving market town possessing a Ladies' Book Club and Assembly Rooms where balls and concerts were held throughout the winter months. Early in 1812, following the deaths of her parents, Maria travelled to Yorkshire to visit her uncle who was headmaster of the Wesleyan Methodist School at Woodhouse Grove, near Leeds. It was here that she met Patrick Brontë, who came to examine the school's pupils in the classics. Following a brief courtship the couple were married on 29 December 1812 at St Oswald's Church, Guiseley, West Yorkshire.

ABOVE Portrait of Mrs Maria Brontë by an unknown artist. According to Elizabeth Gaskell, Mrs Brontë was 'extremely small in person; not pretty, but very elegant, and always dressed with a quiet simplicity of taste, which accorded well with her general character'.

LEFT A sampler stitched by Maria Brontë when she was a young girl; completed on her eighth birthday in 1791.

The couple began married life at Lousy Thorn Farm at Hartshead where Patrick had lodged before his marriage, then moved to Clough House at Hightown, where their two eldest children, Maria and Elizabeth, were born. In 1815 they moved to Thornton, near Bradford, where the four famous Brontë children were born. Despite Maria's continual pregnancies, the family enjoyed a pleasant social life at Thornton, centred on the Firth family at Kipping House and their circle of friends. Elizabeth Firth became a close family friend and was godmother to Elizabeth and Anne Brontë.

Shortly after the family made their final move to Haworth in 1820, Mrs Brontë was taken ill with what is believed to have been cancer of the uterus.

> Surely after this you can have no doubt that you possess all my heart. Two months ago I could not possibly have believed that you would ever engross so much of my thoughts and affections, and far less could I have thought that I should be so forward as to tell you so … I feel that my heart is more ready to attach itself to earth than heaven.
>
> *Maria Branwell in a letter to Patrick Brontë, 3 October 1812*

> *Papa put into my hands a little packet of letters and papers – telling me that they were Mama's and that I might read them – I did read them in a frame of mind I cannot describe – the papers were yellow with time all having been written before I was born – it was strange to peruse now for the first time the records of a mind whence my own sprang – and most strange – and at once sad and sweet to find that mind of a truly fine, pure and elevated order … I wished She had lived and that I had known her.*

She died on 15 September 1821 at the age of 38, with her six little children at her bedside.

During their time at Thornton, Maria wrote an essay, *The Advantages of Poverty in Religious Concerns*, which was preserved by Mr Brontë. Although the views expressed in the essay may seem naïve today, possibly its greatest significance lies in the example it set to her daughters of a woman writing with a view to publication. Patrick Brontë also preserved the letters Maria had written to him during their courtship, and long after Maria's death he gave Charlotte her mother's letters to read:

Schooling ... and Tragedy

'A plain and useful Education'

In 1823 the Clergy Daughters' School opened at Cowan Bridge, near Kirkby Lonsdale in Lancashire. The *Leeds Intelligencer* of 4 December 1823 advertised the school as offering the daughters of impoverished clergymen a 'plain and useful Education', with the option of additional accomplishments that would equip them to become teachers or governesses. The cost of board and education was heavily subsidised by an impressive list of patrons, headed by the school's founder, the Revd William Carus Wilson. The school must have seemed like the answer to a prayer for Patrick Brontë, widowed and with six young children to educate on a limited income.

In 1824 Maria and Elizabeth were sent to the school, soon afterwards followed by Charlotte and Emily. The school registers show that the Brontë sisters, with the exception of Elizabeth, were to receive the higher level of education which would equip them to become governesses. It would appear that Elizabeth had been selected to become the family housekeeper, making the additional accomplishments unnecessary in her case. The school regime was harsh, and Charlotte's descriptions of Lowood School in her novel *Jane Eyre* were drawn from her time at Cowan Bridge. Former pupils who attended the school at the same time as the Brontës remembered how Maria was persecuted by a teacher there, and how she suffered without complaint. One of the few surviving accounts of Elizabeth was provided by the superintendent of the school, and relates to a mysterious accident she suffered there:

ABOVE The Clergy Daughters' School at Cowan Bridge, from an engraving of 1824.

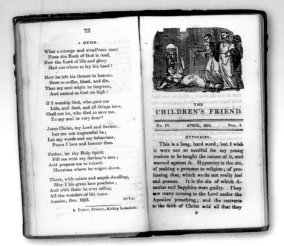

ABOVE *The Child's First Tales* is one of several publications produced by the Revd William Carus Wilson, founder of the Clergy Daughters' School. The text, accompanied by gruesome woodcut illustrations of punishment and death, reveals a preoccupation with infant mortality.

Reads tolerably – Writes indifferently – Ciphers a little and works neatly. Knows nothing of Grammar, Geography, History or Accomplishments. Altogether clever of her age but knows nothing systematically

Extract from the entry for Charlotte Brontë in the registers of Cowan Bridge School

The second, Elizabeth, is the only one of the family of whom I have a vivid recollection, from her meeting with a somewhat alarming accident, in consequence of which I had her for some days and nights in my bed-room, not only for the sake of her greater quiet, but that I might watch over her myself. Her head was severely cut, but she bore all the consequent suffering with exemplary patience, and by it won much upon my esteem.

In the winter of 1824 an epidemic of 'low fever' (typhus) broke out in the school and many pupils became ill. By February 1825 Maria was ill with consumption and Mr Brontë was summoned to take his daughter home. Maria died at the Parsonage on 6 May 1825, aged 11, and was buried in the family vault beside her mother. Elizabeth was also ill, and news of Maria's death prompted the school authorities to send her home. Patrick was so shocked by her condition that he removed Charlotte and Emily from the school. They arrived back at Haworth in time to witness Elizabeth's death on 15 June, at the age of 10. Charlotte's friend, Ellen Nussey, recalled how she would often speak about her dead sisters:

She described Maria as a little mother amongst the rest, superhuman in goodness and cleverness. But most touching of all were the revelations of her sufferings … Charlotte would still weep and suffer when thinking of her. She talked of Elizabeth also, but never with the anguish of expression which accompanied her recollections of Maria.

Charlotte's sense of loss stayed with her for the rest of her life. She later took her revenge: Maria was immortalized as the saintly Helen Burns in *Jane Eyre*, whilst Cowan Bridge became the infamous Lowood School.

ABOVE These faded samplers from 1822 are the only surviving relics of Maria and Elizabeth, the two eldest Brontë children. Maria's was completed on 18 May when she was eight years old, and Elizabeth's on 22 July when she was seven.

Family Life

'... after tea I either read, write, do a little fancy work ...'

Following the deaths of Maria and Elizabeth, the remaining Brontë children gradually settled back into the routines of Parsonage life. Mrs Brontë's elder sister, Elizabeth Branwell, made her home with the Brontë family at Haworth, supervising the running of the household and instilling a keen sense of order into their lives. Mrs Gaskell claimed that 'people in Haworth have assured me that, according to the hour of the day – nay, the very minute – could they have told what the inhabitants of the parsonage were about'. Sarah Garrs, a young servant in the Brontë household who accompanied the family from Thornton, later provided domestic details of the family's early life at Haworth, which changed very little over the years. After morning prayers and a breakfast of porridge, milk, and bread and butter, the children were given lessons by their

ABOVE A painting by Emily of her dog Keeper, dated 24 April 1838. Keeper was a bull mastiff with a ferocious reputation; he died in December 1851 and was buried in the Parsonage garden.

father. The interval between lessons and lunch was spent in learning the rudiments of sewing with Sarah. Lunch was a simple meal of roast or boiled meat and potatoes followed by milk pudding. In the afternoon they walked out on the moors, coming home to tea in the kitchen, followed by 'oral lessons' and discussions with their father before evening prayers and bed.

When at home, the Brontë sisters were expected to take a share of the domestic chores, and Emily in particular was often found in the kitchen, assisting Tabby, a servant, and baking the family's bread. The girls were well-trained in the household arts by their Aunt Branwell. They became skilled at sewing and embroidery, and were all keen, talented visual artists. These 'accomplishments' were essential for the role of governess but also formed a regular part of their day-to-day lives at home. In 1832, after Charlotte returned from her second boarding school, Roe Head, she wrote to her new friend Ellen Nussey:

LEFT The old Parsonage at Thornton, where the four famous Brontë children were born.

LEFT Like his sisters, Branwell Brontë was artistically talented, as demonstrated by this caricature self-portrait, *c*.1840.

RIGHT Emily Brontë's diary paper dated 26 June 1837 includes a sketch of herself and Anne seated at the dining room table. The written contents are a wonderful mix of real life and fantasy.

You ask me to give you a description of the manner in which I have passed every day since I have left School: this is soon done as an account of one day is an account of all. In the morning from nine o'clock till half past twelve I instruct my Sisters & draw, then we walk till dinner after dinner I sew till tea-time, and after tea I either read, write, do a little fancy work or draw, as I please. Thus in one delightful, though somewhat monotonous course my life is passed.

Charlotte's conventional account makes no mention of the extraordinary fantasy worlds which absorbed the Brontës. The events which the sisters chronicled in their fictional worlds were just as real to them as the quiet, domestic routine of the Parsonage. They all spent periods of time away from Haworth, but it was at home that their creative lives flourished; in each others' company, and close to the wild moorland landscape that was such a great source of inspiration to them. In *Jane Eyre*, for example, Charlotte describes Jane's arrival at Whitcross, where the coachman leaves her alone and lost:

There are great moors behind and on each hand of me; there are waves of mountains far beyond that deep valley at my feet. The population here must be thin, and I see no passengers on these roads: they stretch out east, west, north, and south – white, broad, lonely; they are all cut in the moor, and the heather grows deep and wild to their very verge.

ABOVE A portrait of Anne Brontë by her sister Charlotte, dated 17 April 1833.

… I am in the kitchin of the parsonage house Hawarth Taby [sic] the servent is washing up after Breakfast and Anne my youngest Sister (Maria was my eldest) is kneeling on a chair looking at some cakes whiche Tabby has been Baking for us. Emily is in the parlour brushing it papa and Branwell are gone …

Charlotte Brontë, The History of the Year, *12 March 1829*

Imaginary Worlds

'... we were Ronald Macelgin, Henry Angora, Juliet Augusteena ...'

The young Brontës created a rich imaginary world sparked by their father's gift to Branwell of a set of toy soldiers in June 1826. Each of the children adopted a soldier and invested him with a name and character. They created a sequence of plays and stories around the soldiers, or 'The Twelves', as they became known. These were the 'Young Men's Play', 'Our Fellows Play' and 'The Islanders Play'. The Twelves and their imaginary kingdom were presided over by the children in the guise of four powerful genii and their adventures were chronicled in tiny hand-written books, designed to be small enough for the toy soldiers to 'read'. The books were intended to look like printed magazines such as the monthly journal *Blackwood's*, which was an important influence

ABOVE One of the little books produced by the Brontës for their toy soldiers. The books, written with quill pens, contain stories, poetry and reviews and were intended to resemble printed magazines.

on all the Brontë children. The little books contain contents pages and advertisements, and are hand-sewn into covers made from scraps of wallpaper and even old sugar bags. Some of the books are as small as 36 x 55mm, and the miniscule handwriting used makes them difficult to read without the aid of a magnifying glass. Mrs Gaskell was the first person outside the family circle to read these early manuscripts and she found them to be 'the wildest & most incoherent things ... They give one the idea of creative power carried to the verge of insanity.'

ABOVE *Zenobia Marchioness Ellrington*, a pencil drawing by Charlotte Brontë, dated 15 October 1833. Zenobia was an important character in the Brontës' early writings; she was a strong, passionate woman and forerunner of the Brontë heroines to come.

> Papa bought Branwell some soldiers at Leeds when papa came home it was night and we where [sic] in Bed so next morning Branwell came to our Door with a Box of soldiers Emily and I jumped out of Bed and I snathed [sic] up one and exclaimed this is the Duke of Wellington it shall be mine!!
>
> *Charlotte Brontë, The History of the Year, 12 March 1829*

During our excursion we were Ronald Macelgin, Henry Angora, Juliet Augusteena, Rosobelle Esraldan, Ella and Julian Egramont Catherine Navarre and Cordelia Fitzaphnold escaping from the Palaces of Instruction to join the Royalists who are hard driven at present by the victorious Republicans.

We know that many prose works on Gondal were produced by Emily and Anne, but unlike the Angrian chronicles they have not survived. The only clues to Gondal are to be found in the sisters' poetry, diary papers and other fragments. A study of the Brontës' early writings makes clear that elements of the fictional worlds of Angria and Gondal carried over into the published novels of Charlotte, Emily and Anne.

Over the years the Brontës' fantasy world grew in complexity, taking inspiration from every available source. Growing numbers of leading men, based on contemporary heroes and villains, were added to the plays. The Twelves travelled to Africa and founded the fictional Glass Town, which in turn evolved into Angria. Branwell inspired many of his sisters' stories, competing with Charlotte for the lead in artistic invention. Emily and Anne, relegated to minor players in the Angrian saga, took advantage of Charlotte's absence at school in 1831 to form their own land of Gondal. This fascination with their fantasy worlds continued into adulthood, although both Charlotte and Branwell made attempts to break free. Emily felt no such necessity and her diary paper for 1845, written when she was nearly 27 years of age, reveals how on a journey to York she and Anne 'played' at being Gondal characters:

Earning a Living

'... am I to spend all the best part of my life in this wretched bondage ...'

In January 1831 Charlotte, aged 14, was sent to Miss Wooler's school at Roe Head, Mirfield, West Yorkshire. She worked hard, carrying away a silver medal for achievement when she left the following year. It was at Roe Head that she met her lifelong friends, Mary Taylor and Ellen Nussey. Charlotte eventually returned to the school as a teacher, taking first Emily then Anne as pupils. Lacking fortune and connections meant that the sisters were unlikely to attract a husband to support them. Careers in the professions were not open to women and working-class occupations were also out of the question. The only career option which would not incur a loss of social status was teaching, and over the next few years the sisters spent unhappy periods working away from home as governesses, often overworked and always suffering from homesickness.

Great things were expected of Branwell, the only boy. His family believed that he possessed great artistic talent and that one day he would carve out a glittering career for himself in either art or literature. Ambition and hard work had enabled his father to rise in the world and from childhood Branwell bore the weight of his family's expectations. Branwell's artistic career began and ended in Bradford, where he spent 12 months as a portrait artist in 1838. He preferred socializing with other young artists at the local public houses

ABOVE Anne's pencil drawing, *Roe Head, Mirfield*, c.1835–37.

> The thought came over me am I to spend all the best part of my life in this wretched bondage … Must I from day to day sit chained to this chair prisoned within these four bare walls, while these glorious summer suns are burning in heaven & the year is revolving in its richest glow & declaring at the close of every summer day the time I am losing will never come again?
>
> *Charlotte Brontë's Roe Head journal, 1836*

to completing the few commissions he received, and returned home in debt. After the failure of that venture Branwell accepted a post as tutor to the sons of Mr Postlethwaite at Broughton-in-Furness, Cumbria. For a while he made a success of his post and also managed to write in his spare time, but was eventually dismissed for being 'the worse for drink'. His next employment was as assistant clerk-in-charge at Sowerby Bridge railway station on the outskirts of Halifax. It was not the career his family had hoped for, but to Branwell it was a new and exciting world. Six months later he was promoted further up the line

ABOVE The manuscript of Branwell's poem 'Lydia Gisborne' (the maiden name of Mrs Robinson with whom he was infatuated), dated 1 June 1846.

ABOVE During her time as a teacher at Roe Head School, Charlotte scribbled down her private thoughts on scraps of paper. Although these fragments do not constitute a journal in the usual sense of the word, they are known as the 'Roe Head journal'.

BELOW This drawing by Branwell is of the Monk's House, in the grounds of Thorp Green Hall, where he lodged when he worked as tutor to Edmund Robinson.

at Luddenden Foot. A railway audit of the ledgers revealed a discrepancy in the accounts, and although Branwell was not suspected of theft, he was held responsible for negligence.

In the 1840s Branwell achieved a measure of success when several of his poems appeared in local newspapers, making him the first of the Brontë siblings to see his work in print. Eventually, after his string of failed careers, he became tutor in the Robinson household at Thorp Green Hall near York, where Anne was employed as a governess. Anne decided to leave Thorp Green and returned to Haworth in June 1845, followed shortly after by Branwell, once again dismissed in disgrace for 'proceedings bad beyond expression'. It is alleged that he had embarked on an affair with Mrs Robinson, his employer's wife. Mrs Robinson was widowed shortly after, but when it became clear that she had no intention of marrying him, Branwell turned to drink and drugs. Although he did make further attempts to gain employment, he never worked again.

The Brontës in Brussels

'Such a strong wish for wings ...'

In an attempt to escape the dreary lives of governesses, the sisters decided to set up a school of their own at the Parsonage. Charlotte decided that before they put their plan into action, she and Emily should spend time at a school on the Continent. In February 1842, supported by their Aunt Branwell's money, Charlotte and Emily travelled to Brussels to study at the Pensionnat Heger, a well-respected girls' school. Although the reason Charlotte gave her aunt for wishing to go abroad was to improve their language skills and enhance the prospects of their own school, the full truth seems to be that she had been tempted by descriptions of Brussels in the letters of her friend Mary Taylor, who was already studying there, and longed to spread her wings:

Mary's letter spoke of some of the pictures and cathedrals she had seen ... I hardly know what swelled to my throat as I read her letter – such a vehement impatience of restraint and steady work. Such a strong wish for wings ...

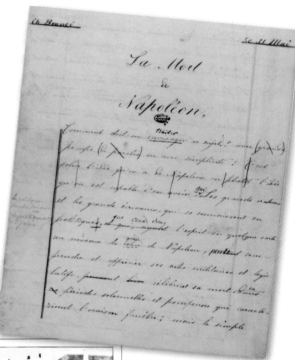

ABOVE Charlotte's fascination with great military leaders is apparent in this essay written during her time in Brussels.

LEFT Charlotte and Emily became pupils at the Pensionnat Heger in Brussels in 1842. The experience of studying here was of great importance in Charlotte's life and work, and two of her four novels, *The Professor* and *Villette*, draw directly on that experience.

ABOVE Charlotte believed herself to be very unattractive and in this illustrated letter from Brussels she has caricatured herself as an ugly, dwarf-like figure.

The sisters remained in Brussels until October, when they were recalled by news from home of their aunt's death. M. Heger wrote to Mr Brontë expressing his regret at losing such exceptional pupils and stressed how given 'another year at most', their studies would have been 'completed and well completed'. Emily decided to remain at the Parsonage as housekeeper, while Charlotte returned to Brussels as a student-teacher. She felt increasingly isolated at the school without Emily's company, and her strong feelings for Heger developed into an obsession. On her return to Haworth in January 1844, Charlotte confided to Ellen Nussey: 'I suffered much before I left Brussels. I think, however long I live, I shall not forget what the parting with M. Heger cost me.' She hoped to combat her unhappiness through hard work, but the school project foundered after a prospectus was circulated and pupils could not be found.

The directress of the school was Madame Zoë Claire Heger. Her husband Constantin taught French literature to the girls and soon became aware of the Brontës' outstanding abilities. He would read great works of literature to Charlotte and Emily, analyse certain passages, then set them to write a piece of their own, 'catching the echo' of the author's style. Heger's influence on Emily is difficult to assess, but his lessons were fundamental to Charlotte's emergence as a great writer.

In half a year, I could acquire a thorough familiarity with French. I could improve greatly in Italian, and even get a dash of German … Papa will perhaps think it a wild and ambitious scheme; but who ever rose in the world without ambition? When he left Ireland to go to Cambridge University, he was as ambitious as I am now. I want us all to go on. I know we have talents, and I want them to be turned to account.

Charlotte Brontë in a letter to Elizabeth Branwell, 29 September 1841

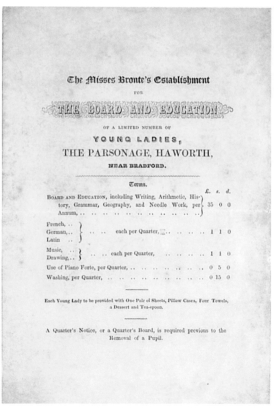

ABOVE The Brontë sisters planned to open a school at Haworth Parsonage so that they could remain together at home and make a living. Their advertisement failed to attract any pupils and the plan was abandoned.

Currer, Ellis and Acton Bell

'Literature cannot be the business of a woman's life ...'

In the autumn of 1845, the Brontë sisters found themselves together at the Parsonage and unemployed. They had been writing prose and poetry since childhood, and as an ambitious 20-year-old, Charlotte had sent samples of her poetry to the Poet Laureate, Robert Southey, telling him of her desire 'to be forever known as a poet', and eliciting the famous response that 'Literature cannot be the business of a woman's life: & it ought not to be'. Although Charlotte kept Southey's letter for the rest of her life, she did not follow his advice.

When Charlotte discovered a notebook containing Emily's poems she was struck by their quality. 'Something more than surprise seized me,' she later wrote, 'a deep conviction that these

ABOVE The signatures of Currer, Ellis and Acton Bell, provided by the Brontës at the request of an early autograph hunter.

were not common effusions, nor at all like the poetry women generally write. I thought them condensed and terse, vigorous and genuine. To my ear, they had also a peculiar music – wild, melancholy and elevating.' Anne had also written poetry and Charlotte found that 'these verses too had a sweet pathos of their own'. She immediately hatched a plan to publish a selection of poems by all three sisters.

Emily was furious at the invasion of her privacy but was eventually won round to the idea of publication. Branwell was not included in the project, despite the fact that he had already had several of his poems published in local newspapers. Charlotte later claimed that he

> Averse to personal publicity, we veiled our own names under those of Currer, Ellis and Acton Bell; the ambiguous choice being dictated by a sort of conscientious scruple at assuming Christian names positively masculine, while we did not like to declare ourselves women …
>
> *Charlotte Brontë*, Biographical Notice of Ellis and Acton Bell, *1850*

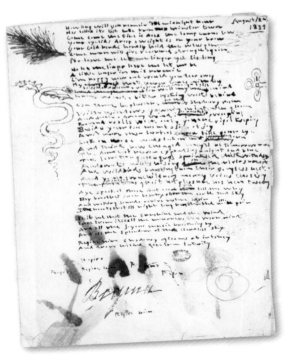

ABOVE A poetry manuscript by Emily, dated 12 August 1839.

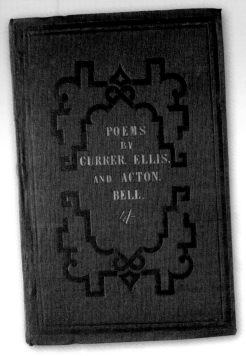

ABOVE Emily Brontë's rosewood writing desk. The contents have been preserved as Emily left them and include blobs of sealing wax, sealing wafers, pen shafts and nibs and a selection of newspaper reviews of *Wuthering Heights*.

LEFT A rare first edition of the Brontë sisters' *Poems*.

never knew of his sisters' publications and was never told, for fear of causing him 'too deep a pang of remorse for his own time misspent, and talents misapplied'. The sisters used a legacy from Aunt Branwell to finance publication and *Poems*, published under the pseudonyms Currer, Ellis and Acton Bell, appeared in 1846. The poems chosen by Anne for inclusion in the volume are often religious in theme, reflecting the influence of William Cowper, a poet she admired. In later years Charlotte was disparaging of her own contribution, dismissing her poems as 'chiefly juvenile productions'. Charlotte's belief in the superiority of Emily's poetry was shared by the critics, but despite some favourable reviews, only two copies of the book were sold, and after a year the sisters sent some of the unsold copies to authors they admired. In a note accompanying one of these copies Charlotte wrote:

My relatives Ellis & Acton Bell and myself, heedless of the repeated warnings of various respectable publishers, have committed the rash act of printing a volume of poems ... our book is found to be a drug; no man needs it or heeds it; in the space of a year our publisher has disposed but of two copies and by what painful efforts he succeeded in getting rid of those two – himself only knows.

Poems by Currer, Ellis and Acton Bell must rank amongst the greatest failures in the history of publishing, but the sisters were determined not to be crushed and each set to work on writing a novel.

ABOVE A draft of a poem by Charlotte which includes a portrait of a young woman in evening dress, and various smaller sketches.

The Brontë Novels

'Read Jane Eyre ... but burn Wuthering Heights.'

The first Brontë novels were published in 1847 following many years of literary activity beginning in childhood. The sisters concealed their true identities, continuing to publish under their pseudonyms: Currer, Ellis and Acton Bell. Charlotte's first attempt to write a novel for publication was *The Professor*. It was rejected by every publisher she sent it to, although the London firm of Smith, Elder & Co recognized the author's potential and sent a letter to her which 'discussed its merits and demerits so courteously that this very refusal cheered the author better than a vulgarly-expressed acceptance would have done'.

> The Bells are of a hardy race. They do not lounge in drawing-rooms or boudoirs. The air they breathe is not that of the hot-house, or perfumed apartments: but it whistles through the rugged thorns that shoot out their prickly arms on barren moors, or it ruffles the moss on the mountain tops.
>
> *A review of* The Tenant of Wildfell Hall, *the* Examiner, *29 July 1848*

ABOVE The manuscript of *Jane Eyre,* which contains one of the most famous opening lines in English literature: 'There was no possibility of taking a walk that day.' The manuscript was bequeathed to the British Museum by Elizabeth Smith, widow of Charlotte's publisher George Smith.

ABOVE The first edition of Emily's *Wuthering Heights* and Anne's *Agnes Grey,* published by Thomas Cautley Newby in 1847.

They added that any future work would 'meet with careful attention'. Charlotte was already working on another novel which was dispatched to the firm a few weeks later. *Jane Eyre* appeared in October 1847 and was instantly popular with the reading public.

Emily's *Wuthering Heights* and Anne's *Agnes Grey* had already been accepted for publication by Thomas Cautley Newby, on terms which Charlotte described as 'somewhat impoverishing to the two authors'. It was agreed that the authors would pay the sum of £50 which Newby undertook to refund when a sufficient number of copies had sold. The two novels were published together

Acton. The works of all three authors were seen as flawed in their depiction of wild characters and violent scenes, although reviewers were forced to acknowledge the power and originality of the Bells' writing, and the books continued to sell.

But within two years both Emily and Anne were dead. Charlotte outlived her sisters by six years and produced two further novels: *Shirley*, published in 1849, and *Villette*, published in 1853. *The Professor* was finally published in 1857, two years after Charlotte's death.

as a three-volume set in December 1847. The phenomenal success of *Jane Eyre* aroused a great deal of speculation over the identity of its author, Currer Bell, which was fuelled by the appearance of further 'Bell' novels. 'And who *is* Currer Bell?' queried the reviewer for the *Critic*, adding, 'The question is asked again and again in every literary coterie in London, at every tea-table in the country. Who are the *three* Bells ... Are they three or one?'

Wuthering Heights and Anne's second novel, *The Tenant of Wildfell Hall*, were considered 'coarse'; 'lady-readers' were warned against them. An anonymous reviewer for *Paterson's Magazine* advised: 'Read *Jane Eyre* ... but burn *Wuthering Heights*'. Reviews of *Jane Eyre*, which had been favourable at first, began to reflect the shocked condemnation levelled at the works of Ellis and

Loss and Legacy

'... stripped and bereaved ...'

Branwell died suddenly on 24 September 1848, aged 31. Soon after, Emily and Anne became ill. In fact both sisters were dying from tuberculosis, and after Branwell's funeral, Emily never left the Parsonage again. She died on 19 December 1848, at the age of 30. Anne was anxious to try a sea cure, and on 24 May 1849, accompanied by Charlotte and Ellen Nussey, she set out for Scarborough, where she died just four days later at the age of 29. To spare her father the anguish of another family funeral, Charlotte had her sister buried in Scarborough, then returned to Haworth alone.

In 1854 Charlotte accepted a proposal from her father's curate, Arthur Bell Nicholls, and the couple were married in Haworth Church on 29 June that year. The marriage was happy, although short-lived. Charlotte Brontë died on 31 March 1855, in the early stages of pregnancy. Mr Brontë lived on at the Parsonage for the remaining six years of his life, cared for by his son-in-law. After the death of Patrick Brontë, Mr Nicholls returned to Ireland, taking many of the Brontës' personal possessions with him. The household goods and furniture were sold at auction, and Mr Brontë's successor, the Revd John Wade, took up residence at the Parsonage.

ABOVE 'A PARODY', Branwell Brontë's last known drawing, made shortly before his death in 1848, shows him being summoned from sleep by Death.

The Brontë Society, formed in 1893, opened a small museum in Haworth two years later, but they always hoped to acquire Haworth Parsonage to house their growing collection of artefacts. Following on from Wade, the Parsonage served as home to three more incumbents before it was bought by a local businessman, Sir James Roberts, who presented it to the Brontë Society in 1928.

Today the Brontë Society continues to care for the family's former home and to carry out its founding aim: to collect, preserve, publish and exhibit material relating to the Brontës' lives and works, and make them known to a wider audience.

A year ago – had a prophet warned me how I should stand in June 1849 – how stripped and bereaved ... I should have thought – this can never be endured.

Charlotte Brontë in a letter to W.S. Williams (the reader at the publishers who first saw the potential in her work), 13 June 1849

ABOVE Anne Brontë's grave in the churchyard of St Mary's, Scarborough, North Yorkshire.